THE GLUGS OF GOSH

By C. J. Dennis

With Illustrations by Hal Gye

ETT Imprint

Exile Bay

This edition published by ETT Imprint, Exile Bay 2022
First electronic edition ETT Imprint 2017

ETT IMPRINT

PO Box R1906

Royal Exchange NSW 1225

Australia

Illustrated edition copyright © ETT Imprint Pty Ltd, 1995, 2020

Introduction copyright © John Derum 1995, 2022

ISBN 978-1-922698-09-4 (pbk) ISBN 978-1-922698-10-0 (ebk)
Cover: Hal Gye
Designed by Tom Thompson

To My Wife

THE CITY OF GOSH

INTRODUCTION

The Glugs of Gosh is a masterpiece. Not just an Australian masterpiece, and not just C. J. Dennis's masterpiece. It is a masterpiece of our language, and it will be a surprise to many people that it was created by a writer still associated with the particularly Australian idiom of his most popular character, The Sentimental Bloke.

The Glugs of Gosh describes the journey of our society in the twentieth century. It is all the more remarkable that it was written and published so early in the 1900s. Dennis could already see the problems in our systems of education, trade, defence and democracy. He was concerned that his earlier work *The Moods of Ginger Mick* had been used to support the case for war, and he was keen to put the record straight about his own view.

In *The Glugs*, Dennis gives us a hero who would be at home much later in the century when we began to understand, at last, our individual spirituality and the significance of our natural environment.

In a comprehensive social satire that touches all of the major social issues, from the nature of government and justice to education and trade, Dennis's observations about domestic possessions are possibly the earliest of the kind that were developed by Barry Humphries so effectively nearly half a century later.

Despite the phenomenal success of *The Songs of A Sentimental Bloke* (1915) and *The Moods of Ginger Mick* (1916), and a universally enthusiastic critical reception, *The Glugs of Gosh* was only moderately well received by the public when it was first published in 1917. Dennis himself was undoubtedly disappointed and is reported to have remarked, 'Oh well, that's for later, when people wake up to themselves. Maybe it'll take on in a hundred years.' The hundred years have not passed but perhaps we have woken up sufficiently to appreciate *The*

Glugs. Nevertheless, it is depressing for aspiring satirists to think that we learn so reluctantly and that the rapier thrust cannot provoke the insensitive target.

Anyone who knows *The Glugs of Gosh* treasures it with a special affection. And for those who are about to discover this delight for the first time, we envy you.

Read *The Glugs* aloud, alone or with others. Read it over and over. Read it on trains and buses and gasp and giggle to the envy of all. Quote it to colleague and competitor, share it with young and old. Relish the rollicking rhythms and the range of exquisite rhymes, for it is easy to miss the skill behind the meticulous construction and the precision in the selection of each word and phrase, when we are swept along by the plot and the characters.

Since I became involved with the writings of C. J. Dennis (in 1976, around the centenary of his birth), I have been in the privileged position of spending many hours with the wealth of material that has been somewhat hidden behind his major successes, *The Sentimental Bloke* and its sequels. I have met many other enthusiasts throughout Australia, and we all agree that, without diminishing in any way The Sentimental Bloke and Mick and Doreen and a score of other characters, *The Glugs of Gosh* is C. J. Dennis's shining hour.

JOHN DERUM
Sydney 2022

CONTENTS

ET him who is minded to meet with a Glug
Pluck three hardy hairs from a rabbit-skin rug;
Blow one to the South, and one to the West,
Then burn another and swallow the rest.
And who shall explain 'tis the talk of a fool,
He's a Glug! He's a Glug of the old Gosh school!
And he'll climb a tree, if the East wind blows,
In a casual way, just to show that he knows . .
      Now, tickle his toes!
      Oh, tickle his toes!
And don't blame me if you come to blows.

                —OLD GOSH RHYME

I. THE GLUG QUEST

OLLOW the river and cross the ford,
Follow again to the wobbly bridge,
 to the left at the notice board,
Climbing the cow-track over the ridge
Tip-toe soft by the little red house,
Hold your breath if they touch the latch,
Creep to the slip-rails, still as a mouse,
Then . . . run like mad for the bracken patch.

Worm your way where the fern fronds tall
  Fashion a lace-work over your head,
Hemming you in with a high, green wall;
  Then, when the thrush calls once, stop dead.
Ask of the old grey wallaby there—
  Him prick-eared by the woollybutt tree—
How to encounter a Glug, and where
  The country of Gosh, famed Gosh may be.

But, if he is scornful, if he is dumb,
Hush! There's another way left. Then come.

On a white, still night, where the dead tree bends
  Over the track, like a waiting ghost,
Travel the winding road that wends
  Down to the shore on an Eastern coast.
Follow it down where the wake of the moon
  Kisses the ripples of silver sand;
Follow it on where the night seas croon
  A traveller's tale to the listening land.

On a white, still night, where the dead tree bends
  Over the track, like a waiting ghost,
Travel the winding road that wends
  Down to the shore on an Eastern coast.
Follow it down where the wake of the moon
  Kisses the ripples of silver sand;
Follow it on where the night seas croon
  A traveller's tale to the listening land.

Step not jauntily, not too grave,
Till the lip of the languorous sea you greet;
Wait till the wash of the thirteenth wave
Tumbles a jellyfish out at your feet.
Not too hopefully, not forlorn,
Whisper a word of your earnest quest;
Shed not a tear if he turns in scorn
And sneers in your face like a fish possessed.

Hist! Hope on! There is yet a way.
Brooding jellyfish won't be gay.

Wait till the clock in the tower booms three,
And the big bank opposite gnashes its doors,
Then glide with a gait that is carefully free
By the great brick building of seventeen floors;
Haste by the draper who smirks at his door,
Straining to lure you with sinister force,
Turn up the lane by the second-hand store,
And halt by the light bay carrier's horse.

By the carrier's horse with the long, sad face
And the wisdom of years in his mournful eye;
Bow to him thrice with a courtier's grace,
Proffer your query, and pause for reply.
Eagerly ask for a hint of the Glug,
Pause for reply with your hat in your hand;
If he responds with a snort and a shrug
Strive to interpret and understand.

Rare will a carrier's horse condescend.
Yet there's another way. On to the end!
Catch the four-thirty; your ticket in hand,
Punched by the porter who broods in his box;
Journey afar to the sad, soggy land,
Wearing your shot-silk lavender socks.
Wait at the creek by the moss-grown log
Till the blood of a slain day reddens the West.

Hark for the croak of a gentleman frog,
Of a corpulent frog with a white satin vest.

Catch the four-thirty; your ticket in hand,
Punched by the porter who broods in his box;
Journey afar to the sad, soggy land,
Wearing your shot-silk lavender socks.
Wait at the creek by the moss-grown log
Till the blood of a slain day reddens the West.
Hark for the croak of a gentleman frog,
Of a corpulent frog with a white satin vest.

Go as he guides you, over the marsh,
  Treading with care on the slithery stones,
Heedless of night winds moaning and harsh
  That seize you and freeze you and search for your bones.
On to the edge of a still, dark pool,
  Banishing thoughts of your warm wool rug;
Gaze in the depths of it, placid and cool,
  And long in your heart for one glimpse of a Glug.

"Krock!" Was he mocking you? "Krock! Kor-r-rock!"
Well, you bought a return, and it's past ten o'clock.

Choose you a night when the intimate stars
  Carelessly prattle of cosmic affairs.
Flat on your back, with your nose pointing Mars,
  Search for the star who fled South from the Bears.
Gaze for an hour at that little blue star,
  Giving him, cheerfully, wink for his wink;
Shrink to the size of the being you are;
  Sneeze if you have to, but softly; then think.

Throw wide the portals and let your thoughts run
  Over the earth like a galloping herd.
Bounds to profundity let there be none,
  Let there be nothing too madly absurd.
Ponder on pebbles or stock exchange shares,
  On the mission of man or the life of a bug,
On planets or billiards, policemen or bears,
  Alert all the time for the sight of a Glug.

Meditate deeply on softgoods or sex,
  On carraway seeds or the causes of bills,
Biology, art, or mysterious wrecks,
  Or the tattered white fleeces of clouds on blue hills.
Muse upon ologies, freckles and fog,
  Why hermits live lonely and grapes in a bunch,
On the ways of a child or the mind of a dog,
  Or the oyster you bolted last Friday at lunch.

Heard you no sound like a shuddering sigh?
Or the great shout of laughter that swept down the sky?
Saw you no sign on the wide Milky Way?
Then there's naught left to you now but to pray.

Sit you at eve when the Shepherd in Blue
  Calls from the West to his clustering sheep.
Then pray for the moods that old mariners woo,
    For the thoughts of young mothers who watch their
          babes sleep.
Pray for the heart of an innocent child,
  For the tolerant scorn of a weary old man,
For the petulant grief of a prophet reviled,
  For the wisdom you lost when your whiskers began.

Pray for the pleasures that he who was you
  Found in the mud of a shower-fed pool,
For the fears that he felt and the joys that he knew
  When a little green lizard crept into the school.
Pray as they pray who are maddened by wine:
  For distraction from self and a spirit at rest.
Now, deep in the heart of you search for a sign—
  If there be naught of it, vain is your quest.

Lay down the book, for to follow the tale
Were to trade in false blame, as all mortals who fail.
And may the gods salve you on life's dreary round;
For 'tis whispered: "Who finds not, 'tis he shall be found!"

II.   JOI, THE GLUG

"THEY CLIMB THE TREES"

HE Glugs abide in a far, far land,
That is partly pebbles and stones and sand,
 But mainly earth of a chocolate hue,
When it isn't purple or slightly blue.
And the Glugs live there with their aunts
      and wives,
  In draught-proof tenements all their lives.
And they climb the trees when the weather is wet,
To see how high they can really get.
     Pray, don't forget,
This is chiefly done when the weather is wet.

And every shadow that flits and hides,
And every stream that glistens and glides
 And laughs its way from a highland height,
 All know the Glugs quite well by sight.
And they say, "Our test is the best by far;
For a Glug is a Glug; so there you are!
And they climb the trees when it drizzles or hails
To get electricity into their nails;
    And the Glug that fails
Is a luckless Glug, if it drizzles or hails."

Now, the Glugs abide in the land of Gosh;
And they work all day for the sake of Splosh.
 For Splosh, the First, is the nation's pride,
 And King of the Glugs, on his uncle's side.
And they sleep at night, for the sake of rest;
For their doctors say this suits them best.
  And they climb the trees, as a general rule,
  For exercise, when the weather is cool.
     They're taught at school
To climb the trees when the weather is cool.

And the whispering grass on the gay green hills,
And every cricket that skirls and shrills,
  And every moonbeam, gleaming white,
  All know the Glugs quite well by sight.
And they say, "It is safe, is the test we bring;
For a Glug is an awfully Gluglike thing.
  And they climb the trees when there's sign of a fog,
  To scan the land for a feasible dog.
        They love to jog
  Thro' dells in quest of a feasible dog."

The Glugs eat meals three times a day
Because their fathers ate that way.
  Their grandpas said the scheme was good
  To help the Glugs digest their food.
And 'tis wholesome food the Glugs have got,
For it says so plain on the tin and pot.
  And they climb the trees when the weather is dry
  To get a glimpse of the pale green sky.
        We don't know why,
  But they like to gaze on a pale green sky.

And every cloud that sails aloft,
And every breeze that blows so soft,
  And every star that shines at night,
  All knozv the Glugs quite well by sight.
For they say, "Our test, it is safe and true;
What one Glug does, the other Glugs do;
  And they climb the trees when the weather is hot,
  For a bird's-eye view of the garden plot.
        Of course, it's rot,
  But they love that view of the garden plot."

At half-past two on a Wednesday morn
A most peculiar Glug was born;
    And, later on, when he grew a man,
    He scoffed and sneered at the Chosen Plan.
"It's wrong!" said this Glug, whose name was Joi.
"Bah!" said the Glugs. "He's a crazy boy!"
    And they climbed the trees, as the West wind stirred,
    To hark to the note of the Guffer Bird.
        It seems absurd,
But they're foolishly fond of the Guffer Bird.

And every reed that rustles and sways
By the gurgling river that plashes and plays,
    And the beasts of the dread, neurotic night
    All know the Glugs quite well by sight.
And, "Why," say they; "It is easily done;
For a dexter Glug's like a sinister one!"
    And they climb the trees. Oh, they climb the trees!
    And they bark their knuckles, and chafe their knees;
    And 'tis one of the world's great mysteries
        That things like these
Get into serious histories.

III.   THE STONES OF GOSH

OW, here is a tale of the Glugs of Gosh,
    And a wonderful tale I ween,
Of the Glugs of Gosh and their great King Splosh,
    And Tush, his virtuous Queen.
And here is a tale of the crafty Ogs,
    In the neighbouring land of Podge;
Of their sayings and doings and plottings and brewings,
    And something about Sir Stodge.
       Wise to profundity,
       Stout to rotundity,
    That was the Knight, Sir Stodge.

Oh, the King was rich, and the Queen was fair,
And they made a very respectable pair.
    And whenever a Glug in that peaceful land,
    Did anything no one could understand,
The Knight, Sir Stodge, he looked in a book,
And charged that Glug with the crime called Crook.
    And the great Judge Fudge, who wore for a hat
    The sacred skin of a tortoiseshell cat,
He fined that Glug for his action rash,
And frequently asked a deposit in cash.
    Then every Glug, he went home to his rest
    With his head in a bag and his toes to the West;
       For they knew it was best,
    Since their grandpas slept with their toes to the West.

But all of the tale that is so far told
    Has nothing whatever to do
With the Ogs of Podge, and their crafty dodge,
    And the trade in pickles and glue.
To trade with the Glugs came the Ogs to Gosh,
    And they said in seductive tones,
"We'll sell you pianers and pickles and spanners
    For seventeen shiploads of stones:
        Smooth 'uns or nobbly 'uns,
        Firm 'uns or wobbly 'uns,
    All that we ask is stones."

And the King said, "What ?" and the Queen said, "Why,
That is awfully cheap to the things I buy!
    For that grocer of ours in the light brown hat
    Asks two and eleven for pickles like that!"
But a Glug stood up with a wart on his nose,
And cried, "Your Majesties! Ogs is foes!"
    But the Glugs cried, "Peace! Will you hold your jaw!
    How did our grandpas fashion the law?"
Said the Knight, Sir Stodge, as he opened his Book,
"When the goods were cheap then the goods they took."
    So they fined the Glug with the wart on his nose
    For wearing a wart with his everyday clothes.
And the goods were bought thro' a Glug named Ghones;
And the Ogs went home with their loads of stones,
    Which they landed with glee in the land of Podge.
        Do you notice the dodge?
    Nor yet did the Glugs, nor the Knight, Sir Stodge.

In the following Summer the Ogs came back
    With a cargo of eight-day clocks,
And hand-painted screens, and sewing machines,
    And mangles, and scissors, and socks.

"THAT GROCER OF OURS"

And they said, "For these excellent things we bring
    We are ready to take more stones;
            And in bricks or road-metal
            For goods you will settle
    Indented by your Mister Ghones."
            Cried the Glugs praisingly,
            "Why, how amazingly
    Smart of industrious Ghones!"

And the King said, "Hum," and the Queen said, "Oo!
That curtain! What a bee-ootiful blue!"
    But a Glug stood up with some very large ears,
    And said, "There is more in this thing than appears!
And we ought to be taxing these goods of the Ogs,
Or our industries soon will be gone to the dogs."
    And the King said, "Bosh! You're un-Gluggish and rude!"
And the Queen said, "What an absurd attitude!"
Then the Glugs cried, "Down with political quacks!
How did our grandpas look at a tax?"
    So the Knight, Sir Stodge, he opened his Book.
    "No tax," said he, "wherever I look."
Then they fined the Glug with the prominent ears
For being old-fashioned by several years;
    And the Ogs went home with the stones, full-steam.
            Do you notice the scheme?
    Nor yet did the Glugs in their dreamiest dream.

Then every month to the land of Gosh
    The Ogs, they continued to come,
With buttons and hooks, and medical books,
    And rotary engines, and rum,
Large cases with labels, occasional tables,
    Hair tonic, and fiddles and 'phones;

And the Glugs, while concealing their joy in the dealing,
　Paid promptly in nothing but stones.
　　　Why, it was screamingly
　　　Laughable, seemingly—
　Asking for nothing but stones!

And the King said, "Haw!" and the Queen said, "Oh!
Our drawing-room now is a heavenly show
　Of large overmantels, and whatnots, and chairs,
　And a statue of Splosh at the head of the stairs!"
But a Glug stood up with a cast in his eye,
And he said, "Far too many such baubles we buy;
　With all the Gosh factories closing their doors,
　And importers' warehouses lining our shores."
But the Glugs cried, "Down with such meddlesome fools!
What did our grandpas lay down in their rules ?"
　And the Knight, Sir Stodge, he opened his Book:
　"To Cheapness," he said, "was the road they took."
Then every Glug who was not too fat
Turned seventeen handsprings, and jumped on his hat.
　They fined the Glug with the cast in his eye
　For looking both ways—which he did not deny—
And for having no visible precedent, which
Is a crime in the poor and a fault in the rich.

So the Glugs continued, with greed and glee,
To buy cheap clothing, and pills, and tea;
　Till every Glug in the land of Gosh
　Owned three clean shirts and a fourth in the wash.
But they all grew idle, and fond of ease,
And easy to swindle, and hard to please;

And the voice of Joi was a lonely voice,
When he railed at Gosh for its foolish choice.
But the great King grinned, and the good Queen gushed,
As the goods of the Ogs were madly rushed.
And the Knight, Sir Stodge, with a wave of his hand,
Declare it a happy and properous land.

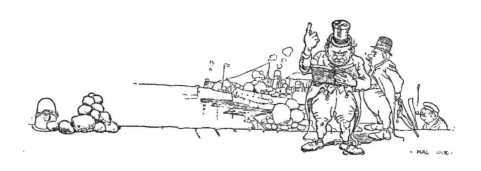

IV.　　SYM, THE SON OF JOI

As Glug blamed Glug.

OW, Joi, the rebel, he had a son
    In far, far Gosh where the tall trees wave.
Said Joi: "In Gosh there shall yet be one
    To scorn this life of a self-made slave;
To spurn the law of the Knight, Sir Stodge,
    And end the rule of the great King Splosh;
Who shall warn the Glugs of their crafty dodge,
    And at last bring peace, sweet peace, to Gosh."

Said he: "Whenever the kind sun showers
His golden treasure on grateful flowers,
    With upturned faces and hearts bowed low,
    The Glugs shall know what the wild things know."
Said he: "Wherever the broad fields smile,
They shall walk with clean minds, free of guile;
    They shall scoff aloud at the call of Greed,
    And turn to their labours and never heed."

So Joi had a son, and his name was Sym;
    And his eyes were wide as the eyes of Truth;
And there came to the wondering mind of him
    Long thoughts of the riddle that vexes youth.
And, "Father," he said, "in the mart's loud din
    Is there aught of pleasure? Do some find joy?"
But his father tilted the beardless chin,
    And looked in the eyes of the questing boy.

Said he: "Whenever the fields are green,
Lie still, where the wild rose fashions a screen,
    While the brown thrush calls to his love-wise mate,
    And know what they profit who trade with Hate."
Said he: "Whenever the great skies spread,
In the beckoning vastness overhead,
    A tent for the blue wren building a nest,
    Then, down in the heart of you, learn what's best."

And there came to Sym as he walked afield
    Deep thoughts of the world and the folk of Gosh.
He saw the idols to which they kneeled;
    He marked them cringe to the name of Splosh.
"Is it meet," he asked, "that a soul should crawl
    To a purple robe or a gilded chair?"
But his father walked to the garden's wall
    And stooped to a rose-bush flowering there.

Said he: "Whenever a bursting bloom
Looks up to the sun, may a soul find room
    For a measure of awe at the wondrous birth
    Of one more treasure to this glad earth."
Said he: "Whenever a dewdrop clings
To a gossamer thread, and glitters and swings,
    Deep in humility bow your head
    To a thing for a blundering mortal's dread."

And there came to Sym in his later youth,
    With the first clear glance in the face of guile,
Thirst for knowledge and thoughts of truth,
    Of gilded baubles, and things worth while.
And he said, "There is much that a Glug should know;
    But his mind is clouded, his years are few."
Then Joi, the father, he answered low,
    As his thoughts ran back to the youth he knew.

Said he: "Whenever the West wind stirs,
And birds in feathers and beasts in furs
　　Steal out to dance in the glade, lie still :
　　Let your heart teach you what it will."
Said he: "Whenever the moonlight creeps
Thro' inlaced boughs, and a shy star peeps
　　Adown from its crib in the cradling sky,
　　Know of their folly who fear to die."

New interest came to the mind of Sym,
　　As 'midst his fellows he lived and toiled.
But the ways of the Glug folk puzzled him;
　　For some won honour, while some were foiled;
Yet all were filled with a vague unrest
　　As they climbed their trees in an endless search.
But Joi, the father, he mocked their quest,
　　When he marked a Glug on his hard-won perch.

Said he: "Whenever these tales are heard
Of the Feasible Dog or the Guffer Bird,
　　Then laugh and laugh till the fat tears roll
　　To the roots of the joy-bush deep in your soul.
When you see them squat on the tree-tops high,
Scanning for ever that heedless sky,
　　Lie flat on your back on the good, green earth
　　And roar till the great vault echoes your mirth."

As he walked in the city, to Sym there came
　　Sounds envenomed with fear and hate,
Shouts of anger and words of shame,
　　As Glug blamed Glug for his woeful state.
"This blame?" said Sym, "Is it mortal's right
　　To blame his fellow for aught he be ?"
But the father said, "Do we blame the night
　　When darkness gathers and none can see ?"

Said he: "Whenever there springs from earth
A plant all crooked and marred at birth,
   Shall we, unlearned in the Gardener's scheme,
   Blame plant or earth for the faults that seem ?"
Said he: "Whenever your wondering eyes
Look out on the glory of earth and skies,
   Shall you, 'mid the blessing of fields a-bloom,
   Fling blame at the blind man, prisoned in gloom

So Joi had a son, and his name was Sym;
   Far from the ken of the great King Splosh.
And small was the Glugs' regard of him,
   Mooning along in the streets of Gosh.
But many a creature by field and ford
   Shared in the schooling of that strange boy,
Dreaming and planning to gather and hoard
   Knowledge of all things precious to Joi.

V. THE GROWTH OF SYM

"And now," said the teacher . . .

OW, Sym was a Glug; and 'tis mentioned so
That the tale reads perfectly plain as we go.
　　In his veins ran blood of that stupid race
　　Of docile folk, who inhabit the place
Called Gosh, sad Gosh, where the tall trees sigh
With a strange, significant sort of cry
When the gloaming creeps and the wind is high.

When the deep shades creep and the wind is high
The trees bow low as the gods ride by:
　　Gods of the gloaming, who ride on the breeze,
　　Stooping to hearten the birds and the trees.
But each dull Glug sits down by his door,
And mutters, "'Tis windy!" and nothing more,
Like the long-dead Glugs in the days of yore.

When Sym was born there was much to-do,
And his parents thought him a joy to view;
　　But folk not prejudiced saw the Glug,
　　As his nurse remarked, "In the cut of his mug."
For he had their hair, and he had their eyes,
And the Glug expression of pained surprise,
And their predilection for pumpkin pies.

And his parents' claims were a deal denied
By his maiden aunt on his mother's side,
　　A tall Glug lady of fifty-two
　　With a slight moustache of an auburn hue.
"Parental blither!" she said quite flat.
"He's an average Glug; and he's red and fat!
And exceedingly fat and red at that!"

But the father, Joi, when he gazed on Sym,
Dreamed great and wonderful things for him.
   Said he, "If the mind of a Glug could wake
   Then, Oh, what a wonderful Glug he'd make!
We shall teach this laddie to play life's game
With a different mind and a definite aim:
A Glug in appearance, yet not the same."

But the practical aunt said, "Fudge! You fool!
We'll pack up his dinner and send him to school.
   He shall learn about two-times and parsing and capes,
   And how to make money with inches on tapes.
We'll apprentice him then to the drapery trade,
Where, I've heard it reported, large profits are made;
Besides, he can sell us cheap buttons and braid."

So poor young Sym, he was sent to school,
Where the first thing taught is the Golden Rule.
   "Do unto others," the teacher said . . .
   Then suddenly stopped and scratched his head.
"You may look up the rest in a book," said he.
"At present it doesn't occur to me;
But do it, whatever it happens to be."

"And now," said the teacher, "the day's task brings
Consideration of practical things.
   If a man makes a profit of fifteen pounds
   On one week's takings from two milk rounds,
How many . . ." And Sym went dreaming away
To the sunlit lands where the field-mice play,
And wrens hold revel the livelong day.

He walked in the welcoming fields alone,
While from far, far away came the pedagogue's drone
    "If a man makes ... Multiply ... Abstract nouns ...
    From B take ... Population of towns ...
Rods, poles or perches . . . Derived from Greek . . ."
Oh, the hawthorn buds came out this week,
And robins are nesting down by the creek.

So Sym was head of his class not once;
And his aunt repeatedly dubbed him "Dunce."
    But, "Give him a chance," said his father, Joi.
    "His head is abnormally large for a boy."
But his aunt said, "Piffle! It's crammed with bosh!
Why, he don't know the rivers and mountains of Gosh,
Nor the names of the nephews of good King Splosh!"

In Gosh, when a youth gets an obstinate look,
And copies his washing-bill into a book,
    And blackens his boot-heels, and frowns at a joke,
    "Ah. he's getting sense," say the elderly folk.
But Sym, he would laugh when he ought to be sad;
Said his aunt, "Lawk-a-mussy! What's wrong with the lad?
    He romps with the puppies, and talks to the ants,
    And keeps his loose change in his second-best pants,
    And stumbles all over my cauliflow'r plants!"

"There is wisdom in that," laughed the father, Joi.
But the aunt said, "Toity!" and, "Drat the boy!"
    "He shall play," said the father, "some noble part.
    Who knows but it may be in letters or art?
'Tis a dignified business to make folk think."
But the aunt cried, "What! Go messing with ink?
And smear all his fingers, and take to drink?
Paint hussies and cows, and end in the clink ?"

So the argument ran; but one bright Spring day
Sym settled it all in his own strange way.
   "'Tis a tramp," he announced, "I've decided to be;
   And I start next Monday at twenty to three . . ."
When the aunt recovered she screamed, "A tramp ?
A low-lived, pilfering, idle scamp,
Who steals people's washing, and sleeps in the damp ?"

Sharp to the hour Sym was ready and dressed.
"Young birds," sighed the father, "must go from the nest.
   When the green moss covers those stones you tread,
   When the green grass whispers above my head,
Mark well, wherever your path may turn,
They have reached the valley of peace who learn
That wise hearts cherish what fools may spurn."

So Sym went off; and a year ran by,
And the father said, with a smile-masked sigh,
   "It is meet that the young should leave the nest."
   Said the aunt, "Don't spill that soup on your vest!
Nor mention his name! He's our one disgrace!
And he's probably sneaking around some place
With fuzzy black whiskers all over his face."

But, under a hedge, by a flowering peach,
A youth with a little blue wren held speech.
   With his back to a tree and his feet in the grass,
   He watched the thistle-down drift and pass,
And the cloud-puffs, borne on a lazy breeze,
Move by on their errand, above the trees,
Into the vault of the mysteries.

"Now, teach me, little blue wren," said he.
"'Tis you can unravel this riddle for me.
    I am 'mazed by the gifts of this kindly earth.
    Which of them all has the greatest worth?"
He flirted his tail as he answered then,
He bobbed and he bowed to his coy little hen:
"Why, sunlight and worms!" said the little blue wren.

"THEY HANGED POOR JOI"

VI.   THE END OF JOI

HEY climbed the trees ... As was told before,
The Glugs climbed trees in the days of yore,
　　When the oldest tree in the land to-day
　　Was a tender little seedling—Nay,
This climbing habit was old, so old
That even the cheeses could not have told
When the past Glug people first began
To give their lives to the climbing plan.
　　　　And the legend ran
That the art was old as the mind of man.

And even the mountains old and hoar,
And the billows that broke on Gosh's shore
　　Since the far-off neolithic night,
　　All knew the Glugs quite well by sight.
And they tell of a perfectly easy way:
For yesterday's Glug is the Glug of to-day.
　　And they climb the trees When the thunder rolls,
　　To solemnly salve their shop-worn souls.
　　　　For they fear the coals
That threaten to frizzle their shop-worn souls.

They climbed the trees. 'Tis a bootless task
To say so over again, or ask
　　The cause of it all, or the reason why
　　They never felt happier up on high.
For Joi asked why; and Joi was a fool,
And never a Glug of the fine old school
　　With fixed opinions and Sunday clothes,
　　And the habit of looking beyond its nose,
　　　　And treating foes
With the calm contempt of the One Who Knows.

And every spider who heaves a line
And trusts to his luck zvhen the day is fine,
   Or reckless swings from an awful height,
   He knows the Glugs quite well by sight.
"You can never mistake them " he will say;
"For they always act in a Gluglike way.
   And they climb the trees when the glass points fair,
   With circumspection and proper care,
         For they fear to tear
   The very expensive clothes they wear."

But Joi was a Glug with a twisted mind
Of the nasty, meditative kind.
   He'd meditate on the modes of Gosh,
   And dared to muse on the acts of Splosh;
He dared to speak, and, worse than that,
He spoke out loud, and he said it flat.
   "Why climb ?" said he. "When you reach the top
   There's nowhere to go, and you have to stop,
         Unless you drop.
   And the higher you are the worse you flop."

And every cricket that chirps at eve,
And scoffs at the folly of fools who grieve,
   And the furtive mice who revel at night,
   All know the Glugs quite well by sight.
For, "Why," they say, " in the land of Gosh
There is no one else who will bow to Splosh.
   And they climb the trees when the rain pelts down
   And feeds the gutters that thread the town;
         For they fear to drown,
   When floods are frothy and waters brown."

Said the Glug called Joi, "This climbing trees
Is a foolish art, and things like these
    Cause much distress in the land of Gosh.
    Let's stay on the ground and kill King Splosh!"
But Splosh, the king, he smiled a smile,
And beckoned once to his hangman, Guile,
    Who climbed a tree when the weather was calm;
    And they hanged poor Joi on a Snufflebust Palm;
        Then they sang a psalm,
    Did those pious Glugs 'neath the Snufflebust Palm.

And every bee that kisses a flow'r,
And every blossom, born for an hour,
    And every bird on its gladsome flight,
    All know the Glugs quite well by sight.
For they say, " 'Tis a simple test we've got:
If you know one Glug, why, you know the lot!" . . .
    So, they climbed a tree in the bourgeoning Spring,
    And they hanged poor Joi with some second-hand string.
        'Tis a horrible thing
    To be hanged by Glugs with second-hand string.

Then Splosh, the king, rose up and said,
"It's not polite; but he's safer dead.
    And there's not much room in the land of Gosh
    For a Glug named Joi and a king called Splosh!"
And every Glug flung high his hat,
And cried, "We're Glugs! and you can't change that!"
    So they climbed the trees, since the weather was cold,
    While the brazen bell of the city tolled
        And tolled, and told
    The fate of a Glug who was over-bold.

And every cloud that sails the blue,
And every dancing sunbeam too,
And every sparkling dewdrop bright
All know the Glugs quite well by sight.
"We tell," say they, "by a simple test;
For any old Glug is like the rest.
And they climb the trees when there's weather about,
In a general way, as a cure for gout;
Tho' some folks doubt
If the climbing habit is good for gout."

So Joi was hanged, and his race was run,
And the Glugs were tickled with what they'd done.
And, after that, if a day should come
When a Glug felt extra specially glum,
He'd call his children around his knee,
And tell that tale with a chuckle of glee.
And should a little Glug girl or boy
See naught of a joke in the fate of Joi,
Then he'd employ
Stern measures with such little girl or boy.

But every dawn that paints the sky,
And every splendid noontide high,
All know the Glugs so well, so well.
'Tis an easy matter, and plain to tell.
For, lacking wit, with a candour smug,
A Glug will boast that he is a Glug.
And they climb the trees, if it shines or rains,
To settle the squirming in their brains,
And the darting pains
That are caused by rushing and catching trains.

VII.   THE SWANKS OF GOSH

The Swanks of Gosh

OME mourn with me for the land of Gosh,
  Oh, weep with me for the luckless Glugs
Of the land of Gosh, where the sad seas wash
The patient shores, and the great King Splosh
    His sodden sorrow hugs;
Where the the fair Queen Tush weeps all the day,
And the Swank, the Swank, the naughty Swank,
        The haughty Swank holds sway —
The most mendacious, ostentaatious,
        Spacious Swank holds sway.

'Tis sorrow-swathed, as I know full well,
  And garbed in gloom and the weeds of woe,
And vague, so far, is the tale I tell;
But bear with me for the briefest spell,
        And surely shall ye know
Of the land of Gosh, and Tush, and Splosh,
  And Stodge, the Swank, the foolish Swank,
        The mulish Swank of Gosh —
The meretricious, avaricious,
        Vicious Swank of Gosh.

Oh, the tall trees bend, and green trees send
  A chuckle round the earth,
And the soft winds croon a jeering tune,
  And the harsh winds shriek with mirth,
And the wee small birds chirp ribald words
  When the Swank walks down the street;
But every Glug takes off his hat,
And whispers humbly, "Look at that!

Hats off! Hats off to the Glug of rank!
Sir Stodge, the Swank, the Lord High Swank!"
Then the East wind roars a loud guffaw,
And the haughty Swank says, "Haw!

His brain is dull, and his mind is dense,
    And his lack of saving wit complete;
But most amazingly immense
Is his inane self-confidence
        And his innate conceit.
But every Glug, and great King Splosh
    Bowed to Sir Stodge, the fuddled Swank,
        The muddled Swank of Gosh —
The engineering, peeping, peering,
        Sneering Swank of Gosh.

In Gosh, sad Gosh, where the Lord Swank lives,
    He holds high rank, and he has much pelf;
And all the well-paid posts he gives
Unto his fawning relatives,
        As foolish as himself.
In offices and courts and boards
    Are Swanks, and   Swanks, ten dozen Swanks,
        And cousin Swanks in hordes —
Inept and musty, dry and dusty,
        Rusty Swanks in hordes.

The clouds so soft, that sail aloft,
    Weep laughing tears of rain;
The blue sky spread high overhead
    Peeps thro' in mild disdain.
All nature laughs and jeers and chaffs
    When the Swank goes out to walk;

"THE LEAVES AROUND HIM DANCE"

But every Glug bows low his head,
And says in tones surcharged with dread,
    "Bow low, bow low, Glugs lean, Glugs fat!"
    But the North wind snatches off his hat,
And flings it high, and shrieks to see
        His ruffled dignity.

They lurk in every Gov'ment lair,
    'Mid docket dull and dusty file,
Solemnly squat in an easy chair,
Penning a minute of rare hot air
        In departmental style.
In every office, on every floor
    Are Swanks, and Swanks, distracting Swanks,
        And Acting-Swanks a score,
And coldly distant, sub-assistant
        Under-Swanks galore.

In peaceful days when the countryside
    Poured wealth to Gosh, and the skies were blue,
The great King Splosh no fault espied,
And seemed entirely satisfied
        With Swanks who muddled thro'.
But when they fell on seasons bad,
    Oh, then the Swanks, the bustled Swanks,
        The hustled Swanks went mad—
The minute-writing, nation-blighting,
        Skiting Swanks went mad.

The tall trees sway like boys at play,
    And mock him when he grieves,
As one by one, in laughing fun,
    They pelt him with their leaves.

And the gay green trees joke to the breeze,
    As the Swank struts proudly by;
But every Glug, with reverence,
Pays homage to his pride immense —
    A homage deep to lofty rank —
    The Swank! The Swank! The pompous Swank! But
the wind-borne leaves await their chance
            And round him gaily dance.

Now, trouble came to the land of Gosh:
    The fear of battle, and anxious days;
And the Swanks were called to the great King Splosh,
Who said that their system would not wash,
            And ordered other ways.
Then the Lord High Swank stretched forth a paw,
And penned a minute re the law,
    And the Swanks, the Swanks, the other Swanks,
            The brother Swanks said, "Haw!"
These keen, resourceful, unremorseful,
            Forceful Swanks said, "Haw!"

Then Splosh, the king, in a royal rage,
    He smote his throne as he thundered, "Bosh!
In the whole wide land is there not one sage
With a cool, clear brain, who'll straight engage
            To sweep the Swanks from Gosh?"
But the Lord High Stodge, from where he stood,
Cried, "Barley! . . . Guard your livelihood!"
    And, quick as light, the teeming Swanks,
            The scheming Swanks touched wood.
Sages, plainly, labour vainly
            When the Swanks touch wood.

The stealthy cats that grace the mats
*   Before the doors of Gosh,*
Smile wide with scorn each sunny morn;
*   And, as they take their wash,*
A sly grimace o'erspreads each face
*   As the Swank struts forth to court.*
But every Glug casts down his eyes,
And mutters, "Ain't 'is 'at a size!
*   For such a sight our gods we thank.*
*   Sir Stodge, the Swank! The noble Swank!"*
But the West wind tweaks his nose in sport;
*   And the Swank struts into court.*

Then roared the King with a rage intense,
   "Oh, who can cope with their magic tricks?"
But the Lord High Swank skipped nimbly hence,
And hid him safe behind the fence
      Of Regulation VI.
And under Section Four Eight O
   The Swanks, the Swanks, dim forms of Swanks,
      The swarms of Swanks lay low —
These most tenacious, perspicacious,
      Spacious Swanks lay low.

Cried the King of Gosh, "They shall not escape!
   Am I set at naught by a crazed buffoon?"
But in fifty fathoms of thin red tape
The Lord Swank swaddled his portly shape,
      Like a large, insane cocoon.
Then round and round and round and round
   The Swanks, the Swanks, the whirling Swanks,
      The twirling Swanks they wound —
The swathed and swaddled, molly-coddled
      Swanks inanely wound.

Each insect thing that comes in Spring
    To gladden this sad earth,
It flits and whirls and pipes and skirls,
    It chirps in mocking mirth
A merry song the whole day long
    To see the Swank abroad.
But every Glug, whoe'er he be,
Salutes, with grave humility
    And deference to noble rank,
    The Swank, the Swank, the swollen Swank;
But the South wind blows his clothes awry,
        And flings dust in his eye.

So trouble stayed in the land of Gosh;
    And the futile Glugs could only gape,
While the Lord High Swank still ruled King Splosh
With laws of blither and rules of bosh,
        From out his lair of tape.
And in cocoons that mocked the Glug
    The Swanks, the Swanks, the under-Swanks,
        The dunder Swanks lay snug.

Then mourn with me for a luckless land,
    Oh, weep with me for the slaves of tape!
Where the Lord High Swank still held command,
And wrote new rules in a fair round hand,
        And the Glugs saw no escape;
Where tape entwined all Gluggish things,
    And the Swank, the Swank, the grievous Swank,
        The devious Swank pulled strings—
The perspicacious, contumacious
        Swank held all the strings.

The blooms that grow, and, in a row,
Peep o'er each garden fence,
They nod and smile to note his style
Of ponderous pretence;
Each roving bee has fits of glee
When the Swank goes by that way.
But every Glug, he makes his bow,
And says, "Just watch him! Watch him now!
He must have thousands in the bank!
The Swank! The Swank! The holy Swank!"
But the wild winds snatch his kerchief out,
And buffet him about.

VIII.   THE SEER

The Seer

OMEWHERE or other, 'tis doubtful where,
In the archives of Gosh is a volume rare,
   A precious old classic that nobody reads,
   And nobody asks for, and nobody heeds;
Which makes it a classic, and famed thro' the
     land,

As well-informed persons will quite understand.

'Tis a ponderous work, and 'tis written in prose,
For some mystical reason that nobody knows;
   And it tells in a style that is terse and correct
   Of the rule of the Swanks and its baneful effect
On the commerce of Gosh, on its morals and trade;
And it quotes a grave prophecy somebody made.

And this is the prophecy, written right bold
On a parchment all tattered and yellow and old;
   So old and so tattered that nobody knows
   How far into foretime its origin goes.
But this is the writing that set Glugs agog
When 'twas called to their minds by the Mayor of Quog:

When Gosh groaneth bastlie thro Greed and bus plannes
Ye ximer shall mende ye who mendes pottes and pans.

Now, the Mayor of Quog, a small suburb of Gosh,
Was intensely annoyed at the act of King Splosh
   In asking the Mayor of Piphel to tea
   With himself and the Queen on a Thursday at three;
When the King must have known that the sorriest dog,
If a native of Piphel, was hated in Quog.

O'er the prophecy pored.

An act without precedent! Quog was ignored!
The Mayor and Council and Charity Board,
    They met and considered this insult to Quog;
    And they said, " 'Tis the work of the treacherous Og!
'Tis plain the Og influence threatens the Throne;
And the Swanks are all crazed with this trading in stone."

Said the Mayor of Quog: "This has long been foretold
In a prophecy penned by the Seer of old.
    We must search, if we'd banish the curse of our time,
    For a mender of pots who's 'a maker of rhyme.
'Tis to him we must look when our luck goes amiss.
But, Oh, where in all Gosh is a Glug such as this?"

Then the Mayor and Council and Charity Board
O'er the archival prophecy zealously pored,
    With a pursing of lips and a shaking of heads,
    With a searching and prying for possible threads
That would lead to discover this versatile Glug
Who modelled a rhyme while he mended a mug.

With a pursing of lips and a shaking of heads,
They gave up the task and went home to their beds,
    Where each lay awake while he tortured his brain
    For a key to the riddle, but ever in vain . . .
Then, lo, at the Mayor's front door in the morn
A tinker called out, and a Movement was born.

"Kettles and pans! Kettles and pans!
Oh, the stars are the gods'; but the earth, it is man's.
    But a fool is the man who has wants without end,
    While the tinker's content with a kettle to mend.
For a tinker owns naught but the earth, which is man's.
Then, bring out your kettles! Ho, kettles and pans!"

From the mayoral bed with unmayoral cries
The magistrate sprang ere he'd opened his eyes.
    "Hold him!" he yelled, as he bounced on the floor.
    "Oh, who is this tinker that rhymes at my door?
Go get me the name and the title of him!"
They answered, "Be calm, sir. 'Tis no one but Sym.

"'Tis Sym, the mad tinker, the son of old Joi,
Who ran from his home when a bit of a boy.
    He went for a tramp, tho' 'tis common belief,
    When folk were not looking he went for a thief;
Then went for a tinker, and rhymes as he goes.
Some say he's crazy, but nobody knows."

'Twas thus it began, the exalting of Sym,
And the mad Gluggish struggle that raged around him.
    For the good Mayor seized him, and clothed him in silk,
    And fed him on pumpkins and pasteurised milk,
And praised him in public, and coupled his name
With Gosh's vague prophet of archival fame.

The Press interviewed him a great many times,
And printed his portrait, and published his rhymes;
    Till the King and Sir Stodge and the Swanks grew afraid
    Of his fame 'mid the Glugs and the trouble it made.
For, wherever Sym went in the city of Gosh,
There were cheers for the tinker, and hoots for King Splosh.

His goings and comings were watched for and cheered;
And a crowd quickly gathered where'er he appeared.
    All the folk flocked around him and shouted his praise;
    For the Glugs followed fashion, and Sym was a craze.
They sued him for words, which they greeted with cheers,
For the way with a Glug is to tickle his ears.

"O, speak to us, Tinker! Your wisdom we crave!"
They'd cry when they saw him; then Sym would look
      grave,
   And remark, with an air, " 'Tis a very fine day."
   "Now ain't he a marvel ?" they'd shout. "Hip, Hooray!"
"To live," would Sym answer, "To live is to feel!"
"And ain't he a poet?" a fat Glug would squeal.

Sym had a quaint fancy in phrase and in text;
When he'd fed them with one they would howl for the
      next.
   Thus he'd cry, "Love is love!" and the welkin they'd lift
   With their shouts of surprise at his wonderful gift.
He would say "After life, then a Glug must meet death!"
And they'd clamour for more ere he took the next breath.

But Sym grew aweary of this sort of praise,
And he longed to be back with his out-o'-door days,
   With his feet in the grass and his back to a tree,
   Rhyming and tinkering, fameless and free.
He said so one day to the Mayor of Quog,
And declared he'd as lief live the life of a dog.

But the Mayor was vexed; for the Movement had grown,
And his dreams had of late soared as high as a throne.
   "Have a care! What is written is written," said he.
   "And the dullest Glug knows what is written must be.
'Tis the prophet of Gosh who has prophesied it;
And 'tis thus that 'tis written by him who so writ:

"'Lo, the Tinker of Gosh he shall make him three rhymes:
One on the errors and aims of his times,
   One on the symptoms of sin that he sees,
   And the third and the last on whatever he please.

And when the Glugs hear them and mark what they mean
The land shall be purged and the nation made clean.'"

So Sym gave a promise to write then and there
Three rhymes to be read in the Great Market Square
To all Glugs assembled on Saturday week.
"And then," said the Mayor, "if still you must seek
    To return to your tramping, well, just have your fling;
    But I'll make you a marquis, or any old thing . .
    Said Sym, "I shall tinker, and still be a king."

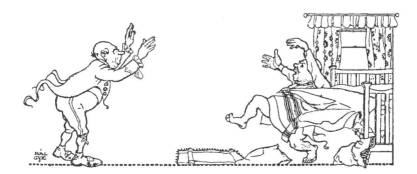

IX.   THE RHYMES OF SYM

OBODY knew why it should be so;
Nobody knew or wanted to know.
  It might have been checked had but some-
body dared
    To trace its beginnings; but nobody cared.
But 'twas clear to the wise that the Glugs of
those days
Were crazed beyond reason concerning a craze.

They would pass a thing by for a week or a year,
With an air apathetic, or maybe a sneer:
  Some ev'ryday thing, like a crime or a creed,
  A mode or a movement, and pay it small heed,
Till Somebody started to laud it aloud;
Then all but the Nobodies followed the crowd.

Thus, Sym was a craze; tho', to give him his due,
He would rather have strayed from the popular view.
  But once the Glugs had him they held him so tight
  That he could not be nobody, try as he might.
He had to be Somebody, so they decreed.
For Craze is an appetite, governed by Greed.

So on Saturday week to the Great Market Square
Came every Glug who could rake up his fare.
  They came from the suburbs, they came from the town,
  There came from the country Glugs bearded and brown,
Rich Glugs, with cigars, all well-tailored and stout,
Jostled commonplace Glugs who dropped aitches about.

There were gushing Glug maids, well aware of their charms,
And stern, massive matrons with babes in their arms.
  There were querulous dames who complained of the
      "squash,"
  The pushing and squeezing; for, briefly, all Gosh,
With its aunt and its wife, stood agape in the ranks —
Excepting Sir Stodge and his satellite Swanks.

The Mayor of Quog took the chair for the day;
And he made them a speech, and he ventured to say
  That a Glug was a Glug, and the Cause they held dear
  Was a very dear Cause. And the Glugs said, "Hear, hear."
Then Sym took the stage to a round of applause
From thousands who suddenly found they'd a Cause.

THE FIRST RHYME OF SYM

We strive together in life's crowded mart,
  Keen-eyed, with clutching hands to over-reach.
We scheme, we lie, we play the selfish part,
  Masking our lust for gain with gentle speech;
And masking too — O pity ignorance!—
Our very selves behind a careless glance.

Ah, foolish brothers, seeking e'er in vain
  The one dear gift that lies so near at hand;
Hoping to barter gold we meanly gain
  For that the poorest beggar in the land
Holds for his own, to hoard while yet he spends;
Seeking fresh treasure in the hearts of friends.

We preach; yet do we deem it worldly-wise
  To count unbounded brother-love a shame,
So, ban the brother-look from out our eyes,
  Lest sparks of sympathy be fanned to flame.

We smile; and yet withhold, in secret fear,
The word so hard to speak, so sweet to hear —

The Open Sesame to meanest hearts,
    The magic word, to which stern eyes grow soft,
And crafty faces, that the cruel marts
    Have seared and scored, turn gentle —
Nay, how oft It trembles on the lip to die unspoke,
And dawning love is stifled with a joke.

Nay, brothers, look about your world to-day:
    A world to you so drab, so commonplace —
The flowers still are blooming by the way,
    As blossom smiles upon the sternest face.
In every hour is born some thought of love;
In every heart is hid some treasure-trove.

With a modified clapping and stamping of feet
The Glugs mildly cheered him, as Sym took his seat.
    But some said 'twas clever, and some said 'twas grand—
    More especially those who did not understand.
And some said, with frowns, tho' the words sounded plain,
Yet it had a deep meaning they craved to explain.

But the Mayor said: Silence! He wished to observe
That a Glug was a Glug; and in wishing to serve
    This glorious Cause, which they'd asked him to lead,
    They had proved they were Glugs of the noble old breed
That made Gosh what it was . . . and he'd ask the police
To remove that small boy while they heard the next piece.

THE SECOND RHYME OF SYM

"Now come," said the Devil, he said to me,
With his swart face all a-grin,
"This day, ere ever the clock strikes three,
Shall you sin your darling sin.
For I've wagered a crown with Beelzebub,
Down there at the Gentlemen's Brimstone Club,
I shall tempt you once, I shall tempt you twice,
Yet thrice shall you fall ere I tempt you thrice."

"Begone, base Devil!" I made reply—
"Begone with your fiendish grin!
How hope you to profit by such as I?
For I have no darling sin.
But many there be, and I knozv them well,
All foul with sinning and ripe for Hell.
And I name no names, but the whole world knows
That I am never of such as those."

"How now?" said the Devil. "I'll spread my net,
And I vow I'll gather you in!
By this and by that shall I win my bet,
And you shall sin the sin!
Come, fill up a bumper of good red wine,
Your heart shall sing, and your eye shall shine,
You shall know such joy as you never have known.
For the salving of men was the good vine grown."

"Begone, red Devil!" I made reply.
"Parch shall these lips of mine,
And my tongue shall shrink, and my throat go dry,
Ere ever I taste your wine!

But greet you shall, as I know full well,
A tipsy score of my friends in Hell.
*   And I name no names, but the whole world wots*
*   Most of my fellows are drunken sots."*

"Ah, ha!" said the Devil. "You scorn the wine!
*   Thrice shall you sin, I say,*
To win me a crown from a friend of mine,
*   Ere three o' the clock this day.*
Are you calling to mind some lady fair?
And is she a wife or a maiden rare?
*   " 'Twere folly to shackle young love, hot Youth;*
*   And stolen kisses are sweet, forsooth!"*

"Begone, foul Devil!" I made reply;
*   "For never in all my life*
Have I looked on a woman with lustful eye,
*   Be she maid, or widow, or wife.*
But my brothers! Alas! I am scandalized
By their evil passions so ill disguised.
*   And 1 name no names, but my thanks I give*
*   That I loathe the lives my fellow-men live."*

"Ho, ho!" roared the Devil in fiendish glee.
*   " 'Tis a silver crown I win!*
Thrice have you fallen! O Pharisee,
*   You have sinned your darling sin!"*
"But, nay," said I; "and I scorn your lure.
I have sinned no sin, and my heart is pure.
*   Come, show me a sign of the sin you see!"*
*   But the Devil was gone . . . and the clock struck three.*

With an increase of cheering and waving of hats —
While the little boys squealed, and made noises
      like cats —
  The Glugs gave approval to Sym's second rhyme.
  And some said 'twas thoughtful, and some said
      'twas prime;
And some said 'twas witty, and had a fine end:
More especially those who did *not* comprehend.

And some said with leers and with nudges and shrugs
That, they mentioned no names, but it hit certain Glugs.
  And others remarked, with superior smiles,
  While dividing the metrical feet into miles,
That the thing seemed quite simple, without any doubt,
But the anagrams in it would need thinking out.

But the Mayor said, Hush! And he wished to explain
That in leading this Movement he'd nothing to gain.
  He was ready to lead, since they trusted him so;
  And, wherever he led he was sure Glugs would go.
And he thanked them again, and craved peace for a time,
While this gifted young man read his third and last rhyme.

THE LAST RHYME OF SYM

(To sing you a song and a sensible song is a worthy and
      excellent thing;
But how could I sing you that sort of a song, if there's
      never a song to sing?)
At ten to the tick, by the kitchen clock, I marked him
      blundering by,
With his eyes astare, and his rumpled hair, and his hat
      cocked over his eye.
Blind, in his pride, to his shoes untied, he went with a
      swift jig-jog,

Off on the quest, with a strange unrest, hunting the
  Feasible Dog.
And this is the song, as he dashed along, that he sang
  with a swaggering swing —
(Now how had I heard him singing a song if he hadn't
  a song to sing?)

"I've found the authentic, identical beast!
  The Feasible Dog, and the terror of Gosh!
    I know by the prowl of him.
    Hark to the growl of him!
  Heralding death to the subjects of Splosh.
Oh, look at him glaring and staring, by thunder!
Now each for himself, and the weakest goes under!

"Beware this injurious, furious brute;
  He's ready to rend you with tooth and with claw.
    Tho' 'tis incredible,
    Anything edible
  Disappears suddenly into his maw:
Into his cavernous inner interior
Vanishes ev'rything strictly superior."

He calls it "Woman," he calls it "Wine," he calls it
  "Devils" and "Dice";
He calls it "Surfing" and "Sunday Golf" and names
  that are not so nice.
But whatever he calls it—"Morals" or "Mirth"—he is
  on with the hunt right quick
For his sorrow he'd hug like a gloomy Glug if he
  hadn't a dog to kick.
So any old night, if the stars are right, you will find
  him, hot on the trail
Of a feasible dog and a teasable dog, with a can to tie
  to his tail.

And the song that he roars to the shuddering stars is a
worthy and excellent thing.
(Yet how could you hear him singing a song if there wasn't
a song to sing?)

"I've watched his abdominous, ominous shape
Abroad in the land while the nation has slept,
Marked his satanical Methods tyrannical;
Rigorous, vigorous vigil I kept.
Good gracious! Voracious is hardly the name for it!
Yet we have only our blindness to blame for it.

"My dear, I've autoptical, optical proof
That he's prowling and growling at large in the land.
Hear his pestiferous Clamour vociferous,
Gurgles and groans of the beastliest brand.
Some may regard his contortions as comical.
But I've the proof that his game's gastronomical.

"Beware this obstreperous, leprous beast—
A treacherous wretch, for I know him of old.
I'm on the track of him,
Close at the back of him,
And I'm aware his ambitions are bold;
For he's yearning and burning to snare the superior
Into his roomy and gloomy interior."

Such a shouting and yelling of hearty Bravoes,
Such a craning of necks and a standing on toes
    Seemed to leave ne'er a doubt that the Tinker's last rhyme
    Had now won him repute 'mid the Glugs for all time.
And they all said the rhyme was the grandest they'd heard:
More especially those who had not caught a word.
But the Mayor said: Peace! And he stood, without fear,
As the leader of all to whom Justice was dear.

For the Tinker had rhymed, as the Prophet foretold,
And a light was let in on the errors of old.
For in every line, and in every verse
Was the proof that Sir Stodge was a traitor, and worse!
Sir Stodge (said the Mayor), must go from his place;
And the Swanks, one and all, were a standing disgrace!

For the influence won o'er a weak, foolish king
Was a menace to Gosh, and a scandalous thing!
"And now," said the Mayor, "I stand here to-day
As your leader and friend." And the Glugs said, "Hooray!"

Then they went to their homes in the suburbs and town;
To their farms went the Glugs who were bearded and brown.
Portly Glugs with cigars went to dine at their clubs,
While illiterate Glugs had one more at the pubs.
And each household in Gosh sat and talked half the night
Of the wonderful day, and the imminent fight.

Forgetting the rhymer, forgetting his rhymes,
They talked of Sir Stodge and his numerous crimes.
There was hardly a Glug in the whole land of Gosh
Who'd a lenient word to put in for King Splosh.
One and all, to the mangiest, surliest dog,
Were quite eager to bark for his Worship of Quog.

Forgotten, unnoticed, Sym wended his way
To his lodging in Gosh at the close of the day.
And 'twas there, to his friend and companion of years —
To his little red dog with the funny prick ears —
That he poured out his woe; seeking nothing to hide;
And the little dog listened, his head on one side.

"O you little red dog, you are weary as I.
It is days, it is months since we saw the blue sky.
  And it seems weary years since we sniffed at the
      breeze
  As it hums thro' the hedges and sings in the trees.
These we know and we love. But this city holds fears,
O my friend of the road, with the funny prick ears.
And for what may we hope from his Worship of Quog?"
"Oh, a bone, and a kick," said the little red dog.

II.   THE DEBATE

"'ULTRA VIRES!' THUNDERED STODGE"

The Debate

E was a Glug of simple charm;
He wished no living creature harm.
    His kindly smile like sunlight fell
    On all about, and wished them well.
Yet, 'spite the cheerful soul of Sym,
The great Sir Stodge detested him.

The stern Sir Stodge and all his Swanks —
Proud Glugs of divers grades and ranks,
    With learning and attainments great —
    Had never learned to conquer hate.
And, failing in their A. B. C.,
Were whipt by Master Destiny.

'Twas thus that Gosh's famous schools
Turned out great hordes of learned fools:
    Turned out the ship without a sail,
    Turned out the kite with leaden tail,
Turned out the mind that could not soar
Because of foolish weights it bore.

Because there'd been no father Joi
To guide the quick mind of a boy
    Away from thoughts of hate and blame,
    Wisdom in these was but a name.
But 'mid the Glugs they count him wise
Who walks with cunning in his eyes.

His task well done, his three rhymes writ,
Sym rose at morn, and packed his kit.

"At last!" he cried. "Off and away
To meet again the spendthrift Day,
As he comes climbing in the East,
To bless with largesse man and beast.

"Again the fields where wild things run!
And trees, all spreading to the sun,
   Run not, because, of all things blest,
   Their chosen place contents them best.
O come, my little prick-eared dog!" . . .
But, "Halt!" exclaimed his Nibs of Quog.

"Nay," said the Mayor. "Not so fast!
The day climbs high, but sinks at last.
   And trees, all spreading to the sun,
   Are slain because they cannot run.
The great Sir Stodge, filled full of hate,
Has challenged you to hold debate.

"On Monday, in the Market Square,
He and his Swanks will all be there,
   Sharp to the tick at half-past two,
   To knock the stuffing out of you.
And if your stuffing so be spread,
Then is the Cause of Quog stone dead.

"In this debate I'd have you find,
With all the cunning of your mind,
   Sure victory for Quog's great Cause,
   And swift defeat for Stodge's laws."
"But cunning I have none," quoth Sym.
The Mayor slowly winked at him.

"Ah!" cried his Worship. "Sly; so sly!"
(Again he drooped his dexter eye)
   "I've read you thro'; I've marked you well.
   You're cunning as an imp from Hell . . .
Nay, keep your temper; for I can
Withal admire a clever man.

"Who rhymes with such a subtle art
May never claim a simple part.
   I'll make of you a Glug of rank,
   With something handy in the bank,
And fixed opinions, which, you know,
With fixed deposits always go.

"I'll give you anything you crave:
A great, high headstone to your grave,
   A salary, a scarlet coat,
   A handsome wife, a house, a vote,
A title, or a humbled foe."
But Sym said, "No," and ever, "No."

"Then," shouted Quog, "your aid I claim
For Gosh, and in your country's name
   I bid you fight the Cause of Quog,
   Or be for ever named a dog!
The Cause of Quog, the weal of Gosh
Are one! Amen. Down with King Splosh !"

Sym looked his Worship in the eye,
As solemnly he made reply:
   "If 'tis to serve my native land,
   On Monday I shall be at hand.
But what am I 'mid such great men?"
His Worship winked his eye again . . .

’Twas Monday in the Market Square;
Sir Stodge and all his Swanks were there.
  And almost every Glug in Gosh
  Had bolted lunch and had a wash,
And cleaned his boots, and sallied out
To gloat upon Sir Stodge’s rout.

And certain sly and knowing Glugs,
With sundry nudges, winks and shrugs,
  Passed round the hint that up on high,
  Behind some window near the sky,
Where he could see yet not be seen,
King Splosh was present with his Queen.

“Glugs,” said the chairman. “Glugs of Gosh;
By order of our good King Splosh,
  The Tinker and Sir Stodge shall meet,
  And here, without unseemly heat,
Debate the question of the day,
Which is — However, let me say —

“I do not wish to waste your time.
So, first shall speak this man of rhyme;
  And, when Sir Stodge has voiced his view,
  The Glugs shall judge between the two.
This verdict from the folk of Gosh
Will be accepted by King Splosh.”

As when, like teasing vagabonds,
The sly winds buffet sullen ponds,
  The face of Stodge grew dark with rage,
  When Sym stepped forth upon the stage.
But all the Glugs, with one accord,
A chorus of approval roared.

Said Sym: "Kind friends, and fellow Glugs;
My trade is mending pots and mugs.
    I tinker kettles, and I rhyme
    To please myself and pass the time,
Just as my fancy wandereth."
("He's mine!" quoth Stodge, below his breath.)

Said Sym: "Why I am here to-day
I know not; tho' I've heard them say
    That strife and hatred play some part
    In this great meeting at the Mart.
Nay, brothers, why should hatred lodge . . ."
"That's ultra vires!" thundered Stodge.

"'Tis ultra vires!" cried the Knight.
"Besides, it isn't half polite.
    And e'en the dullest Glug should know,
    'Tis not pro bono publico.
Nay, Glugs, this fellow is no class.
Remember! Vincit veritas!"

With sidelong looks and sheepish grins,
Like men found out in secret sins,
    Glug gazed at Glug in nervous dread;
    Till one with claims to learning said,
"Sir Stodge is talking Greek, you know.
He may be bad, but never low."

Then those who had no word of Greek
Felt lifted up to hear him speak.
    "Ah, learning, learning," others said.
    'Tis fine to have a clever head."
And here and there a nervous cheer
Was heard, and someone growled, "Hear, hear."

"Kind friends," said Sym ... But, at a glance,
The 'cute Sir Stodge had seen his chance.
   "Quid nunc!" he cried. "O noble Glugs,
   This fellow takes you all for mugs.
I ask him, where's his quid pro quo?
I ask again, quo warranto?

"Shall this man filch our wits from us
With his furor poeticus?
   Nay!" cried Sir Stodge. "You must agree,
   If you will hark a while to me . . ."
And at the Glugs' collective head
He flung strange language, ages dead.

With mystic phrases from the Law,
With many an old and rusty saw,
   With well-worn mottoes, which he took
   Haphazard from the copy-book,
For half an hour the learned Knight
Belaboured them with all his might.

And, as they wakened from their daze,
Their murmurs grew to shouts of praise.
   Glugs who'd reviled him overnight
   All in a moment saw the light.
"O learned man! O seer!" cried they. . . .
And education won the day.

Then, quickly to Sir Stodge's side
There bounded, in a single stride,
   His Nibs of Quog; and flinging wide
   His arms, "O victory!" he cried.
"I'm with Sir Stodge, O Glugs of Gosh!
And we have won! Long live King Splosh!"

Then pointing angrily at Sym,
Cried Quog, "This is the end of him!
 For months I've marked his crafty dodge,
 To bring dishonour to Sir Stodge.
I've lured him here, the traitrous dog,
And shamed him!" quoth his Nibs of Quog.

Hoots for the Tinker tore the air,
As Sym went, wisely, otherwhere.
 Cheers for Sir Stodge were long and loud;
 And, as amid his Swanks he bowed,
To mark his thanks and honest pride,
His Nibs of Quog bowed by his side.

The Thursday after that, at three,
The King invited Quog to tea.
 Quoth Quog, "It was a task to bilk . . .
 (I thank you; sugar, please, and milk) . . .
To bilk this Tinker and his pranks.
A scurvy rogue! . . . (Ah, two lumps, thanks.)

"A scurvy rogue!" continued Quog.
"'Twas easy to outwit the dog.
 Altho', perhaps, I risked my life—
 I've heard he's handy with a knife.
Ah, well, 'twas for my country's sake ...
(Thanks; just one slice of currant cake.)"

XI.   OGS

Ogs

T chanced one day, in the middle of May,
    There came to the great King Splosh
A policeman, who said, while scratching his head,
    "There isn't a stone in Gosh
To throw at a dog; for the crafty Og,
    Last Saturday week, at one,

Took our last blue-metal, in order to settle
    A bill for a toy pop-gun."
        Said the King, jokingly,
        "Why, how provokingly
Weird; but we have the gun."

And the King said, "Well, we are stony-broke."
But the Queen could not see it was much of a joke.
    And she said, "If the metal is all used up,
    Pray what of the costume I want for the Cup?
It all seems so dreadfully simple to me.
The stones? Why, import them from over the sea."

    But a Glug stood up with a mole on his chin,
    And said, with a most diabolical grin,
"Your Majesties, down in the country of Podge,
A spy has discovered a very 'cute dodge.
    And the Ogs are determined to wage a war
    On Gosh, next Friday, at half-past four."
Then the Glugs all cried, in a terrible fright,
"How did our grandfathers manage a fight?"

Then the Knight, Sir Stodge, he opened his Book,
And he read, "Some very large stones they took,
    And flung at the foe, with exceeding force;
    Which was very effective, tho' rude, of course."
And lo, with sorrowful wails and moans,
The Glugs cried, "Where, Oh, where are the stones?"
    And some rushed North, and a few ran West;
    Seeking the substitutes seeming best.
And they gathered the pillows and cushions and rugs
From the homes of the rich and middle-class Glugs.
    And a hasty message they managed to send
    Craving the loan of some bricks from a friend.

On the Friday, exactly at half-past four,
    Came the Ogs with triumphant glee.
And the first of their stones hit poor Mister Ghones,
    The captain of industry.
Then a pebble of Podge took the Knight, Sir Stodge,
    In the curve of his convex vest.
He gurgled "Un-Gluggish!" His heart growing sluggish,
    He solemnly sank to rest.
        'Tis inconceivable,
        Scarcely believable,
    Yet, he was sent to rest.

And the King said, "Ouch!" And the Queen said, "Oo!
My bee-ootiful drawing-room! What shall I do?"
    But the warlike Ogs, they hurled great rocks
    Thro' the works of the wonderful eight-day clocks
They had sold to the Glugs but a month before—
Which was very absurd; but, of course, 'twas war.
    And the Glugs cried, "What would our grandfathers do
    If they hadn't the stones that they one time threw?"
But the Knight, Sir Stodge, and his mystic Book
Oblivious slept in a grave-yard nook.

"THERE ISN'T A STONE IN GOSH"

Then a Glug stood out with a pot in his hand,
As the King was bewailing the fate of his land,
    And he said, "If these Ogs you desire to retard,
    Then hit them quite frequent with anything hard."
So the Glugs seized anvils, and editors' chairs,
And smote the Ogs with them unawares;
    And bottles of pickles, and clocks they threw,
    And books of poems, and gherkins, and glue,
Which they'd bought with the stones — as, of course, you
          know —
From the Ogs but a couple of months ago.
    Which was simply inane, when you reason it o'er;
    And uneconomic, but then, it was war.

When they'd fought for a night and the most of a day,
The Ogs threw the last of their metal away.
    Then they went back to Podge, well content with their fun
    And, with much satisfaction, declared they had won.
And the King of the Glugs gazed around on his land,
And saw nothing but stones strewn on every hand:
    Great stones in the palace, and stones in the street,
    And stones on the house-tops and under the feet.
And he said, with a desperate look on his face,
"There is nothing so ghastly as stones out of place.
    And, no doubt, this Og scheme was a very smart dodge.
    But whom does it profit—my people, or Podge ?"

XII. EMILY ANN

On the royal door-mat.

 OVERNMENT muddled, departments dazed,
Fear and confusion wherever he gazed;
   Order insulted, authority spurned,
   Dread and distraction wherever he turned —
Oh, the great King Splosh was a sad, sore king,
With never a statesman to straighten the thing.

Glugs all importunate urging their claims,
With selfish intent and ulterior aims,
   Glugs with petitions for this and for that,
   Standing ten deep on the royal door-mat,
Raging when nobody answered their ring—
Oh, the great King Splosh was a careworn king.

And he looked to the right, and he glanced to the left,
And he glared at the roof like a monarch bereft
   Of his wisdom and wits and his wealth all in one;
   And, at least once a minute, asked, "What's to be done?"
But the Swanks stood around him and answered, with groans,
"Your Majesty, Gosh is half buried in stones!"

"How now ?" cried the King. "Is there not in my land
One Glug who can cope with this dreadful demand:
   A rich man, a poor man, a beggar man, thief —
   I reck not his rank so he lessen my grief —
A soldier, a sailor, a —" Raising his head,
With relief in his eye, "Now, I mind me!" he said.

"I mind me a Tinker, and what once befel,
When I think, on the whole, he was treated not well.

But he shall be honoured, and he shall be famed
If he read me this riddle. But how is he named?
Some commonplace title, like—Simon?—No—Sym!
Go, send out my riders, and scour Gosh for him."

They rode for a day to the sea in the South,
Calling the name of him, hand to the mouth.
   They rode for a day to the hills in the East,
   But signs of a tinker saw never the least.
Then they rode to the North thro' a whole day long,
And paused in the even to hark to a song.

"Kettles and pans! Kettles and pans!
Oh, who can show tresses like Emily Ann's?
   Brown in the shadow and gold at the tips,
   Bright as the smile on her beckoning lips.
Bring out your kettle! O kettle or pan!
So I buy me a ribband for Emily Ann."

With his feet in the grass, and his back to a tree,
Merry as only a tinker can be,
   Busily tinkering, mending a pan,
   Singing as only a merry man can ...
"Sym!" cried the riders. " 'Tis thus you are styled?"
And he paused in his singing, and nodded and smiled.

Said he: "Last eve, when the sun was low,
Down thro' the bracken I watched her go —
   Down thro' the bracken, with simple grace —
   And the glory of eve shone full on her face;
And there on the sky-line it lingered a span,
So loth to be leaving my Emily Ann."

With hands to their faces the riders smiled.
"Sym," they said —"be it so you're styled —
   Behold, great Splosh, our sorrowing King,
   Has sent us hither, that we may bring
To the palace in Gosh a Glug so named,
That he may be honoured and justly famed."

"Yet," said Sym, as he tinkered his can,
"What should you know of her, Emily Ann ?
   Early as cock-crow yester morn
   I watched young sunbeams, newly born,
As out of the East they frolicked and ran,
Eager to greet her, my Emily Ann."

"King Splosh," said the riders, "is bowed with grief;
And the glory of Gosh is a yellowing leaf.
   Up with you, Tinker! There's work ahead.
   With a King forsaken, and Swanks in dread,
To whom may we turn for the salving of man ?"
And Sym, he answered them, "Emily Ann."

Said he: "Whenever I watch her pass,
With her skirts so high o'er the dew-wet grass,
   I envy every blade the bruise
   It earns in the cause of her twinkling shoes.
Oh, the dew-wet grass, where this morn she ran,
Was doubly jewelled for Emily Ann."

"But haste!" they cried. "By the palace gates
A sorrowing king for a tinker waits.
   And what shall we answer our Lord the King
   If never a tinker hence we bring,
To tinker a kingdom so sore amiss?"
But Sym, he said to them, "Answer him this:

'Every eve, when the clock chimes eight,
I kiss her fair, by her mother's gate:
    Twice, all reverent, on the brow —
    Once for a pray'r, and once for a vow;
Twice on her eyes that they may shine,
Then, full on the mouth because she's mine.'"

"Calf!" sneered the riders. "O Tinker, heed!
Mount and away with us, we must speed.
    All Gosh is agog for the coming of Sym.
    Garlands and greatness are waiting for him:
Garlands of roses, and garments of red,
And a chaplet for crowning a conqueror's head."

"Listen," quoth Sym, as he stirred his fire.
"Once in my life have I known desire.
    Then, Oh, but the touch of her kindled a flame
    That burns as a sun by the candle of fame.
And a blessing and boon for a poor tinker man
Looks out from the eyes of my Emily Ann."

Then they said to him, "Fool! Do you cast aside
Promise of honour, and place, and pride,
    Gold for the asking, and power o'er men—
    Working your will with the stroke of a pen?
Vexed were the King if you ride not with us."
But Sym, he said to them, "Answer him thus:

'Ease and honour and leave to live—
These are the gifts that a king may give . .
    'Twas over the meadow I saw her first;
    And my lips grew parched like a man athirst
Oh, my treasure.was ne'er in the gift of man;
For the gods have given me Emily Ann."

94

"Listen," said they, "O you crazy Sym.
Roses perish, and eyes grow dim.
   Lustre fades from the fairest hair.
   Who weds a woman links arms with care.
But women there are in the city of Gosh —
Ay, even the daughters of good King Splosh . . ."

"Care," said Sym, "is a weed that springs
Even to-day in the gardens of kings.
   And I, who have lived 'neath the tent of the skies,
   Know of the flowers, and which to prize ...
Give you good even! For now I must jog."
And he whistled him once to his little red dog.

Into the meadow and over the stile,
Off went the tinker man, singing the while;
   Down by the bracken patch, over the hill,
   With the little red dog at the heel of him still.
And back, as he soberly sauntered along,
There came to the riders the tail of his song.

"Kettles and pans! Kettles and pans!
Strong is my arm if the cause it be man's.
But a fig for the cause of a cunning old king;
For Emily Ann will be mine in the Spring.
Then naught shall I labour for Splosh or his plans;
Tho' I'll mend him a kettle. Ho, kettles and pans!

XIII. THE LITTLE RED DOG

The Little Red Dog

THE Glugs still live in the land of Gosh,
Under the rule of the great King Splosh.
　　And they climb the trees in the Summer and
　　　　Spring,
　　Because it is reckoned the regular thing.
Down in the Valley they live their lives,
Taking the air with their aunts and wives.

And they climb the trees in the Winter and Fall,
And count it improper to climb not at all.

And they name their trees with a thousand names,
Calling them after their Arts and Aims;
　　And some, they climb for the fun of the thing,
　　But most go up at the call of the King.
Some scale a tree that they fear to name,
For it bears great blossoms of scarlet shame.
　　But they eat of the fruit of the nameless tree,
　　Because they are Glugs, and their choice is free.

But every eve, when the sun goes West,
Over the mountain they call The Blest,
　　Whose summit looks down on the city of Gosh,
　　Far from the reach of the great King Splosh,
The Glugs gaze up at the heights above,
And feel vague promptings to wondrous love.
　　And they whisper a tale of a tinker man,
　　Who lives in the mount with his Emily Ann.

A great mother mountain, and kindly is she,
Who nurses young rivers and sends them to sea.

Taking the air.

And, nestled high up on her sheltering lap,
Is a little red house with a little straw cap
That bears a blue feather of smoke, curling high,
And a bunch of red roses cocked over one eye.
    And the eyes of it glisten and shine in the sun,
    As they look down on Gosh with a twinkle of fun.

There's a gay little garden, a tidy white gate,
And a narrow brown pathway that will not run straight;
    For it turns and it twists and it wanders about
    To the left and the right, as in humorous doubt.
'Tis a humorous path, and a joke from its birth
Till it ends at the door with a wriggle of mirth.
    And here in the mount lives the queer tinker man
    With his little red dog and his Emily Ann..

And, once in a while, when the weather is clear,
When the work is all over, and even is near,
    They walk in the garden and gaze down below
    On the Valley of Gosh, where the young rivers go;
Where the houses of Gosh seem so paltry and vain,
Like a handful of pebbles strewn over the plain;
    Where tiny black forms crawl about in the vale,
    And stare at the mountain they fear them to scale.

And Sym sits him down by his little wife's knee,
With his feet in the grass and his back to a tree;
    And he looks on the Valley and dreams of old years,
    As he strokes his red dog with the funny prick ears.
And he says, "Still they climb in their whimsical way,
While we stand on earth, yet are higher than they.
    Oh, who trusts to a tree is a fool of a man!
    For the wise seek the mountains, my Emily Ann."

So lives the queer tinker, nor deems it a wrong,
When the spirit so moves him, to burst into song.
   'Tis a comical song about kettles and pans,
   And the graces and charms that are Emily Ann's.
'Tis a mad, freakish song, but he sings it with zest,
And his little wife vows it of all songs the best.
   And he sings quite a lot, as the Summer days pass,
   With his back to a tree and his feet in the grass.

And the little red dog, who is wise as dogs go,
He will hark to that song for a minute or so,
   With his head on one side, and a serious air.
   Then he makes no remark; but he wanders elsewhere.
And he trots down the garden to gaze now and then
At the curious pranks of a certain blue wren:
   Not a commonplace wren, but a bird marked for fame
   Thro' a grievance in life and a definite aim.

Now, they never fly far and they never fly high,
And they probably couldn't, suppose they should try.
   So the common blue wren is content with his lot:
   He will eat when there's food, and he fasts when there's not.
He flirts and he flutters, his wife by his side,
With his share of content and forgiveable pride.
   And he keeps to the earth, 'mid the bushes and shrubs,
   And he dines very well upon corpulent grubs.

But the little blue wren with a grievance in life,
He was rude to his neighbours and short with his wife.
   For, up in the apple-tree over his nest,
   There dwelt a fat spider who gave him no rest :
A spider so fat, so abnormally stout
That he seemed hardly fitted to waddle about.
   But his eyes were so sharp, and his legs were so spry,
   That he could not be caught; and 'twas folly to try.

Said the wren, as his loud lamentations he hurled
At the little red dog, "It's a rotten old world!
   But my heart would be glad, and my life would be
         blest
   If I had that fat spider well under my vest.
Then I'd call back my youth, and be seeking to live,
And to taste of the pleasures the world has to give.
   But the world is all wrong, and my mind's in a fog!"
   "Aw, don't be a Glug!" said the little red dog.

Then, up from the grass, where he sat by his tree,
The voice of the Tinker rose fearless and free.

The little dog listened, his head on one side;
Then sought him a spot where a bored dog could hide.

"Kettles and pans! Ho, kettles and pans!
The stars are the gods' but the earth, it is man's!
   Yet down in the shadow dull mortals there are
   Who climb in the tree-tops to snatch at a star:
Seeking content and a surcease of care,
Finding but emptiness everywhere.
   Then make for the mountain, importunate man!
   With a kettle to mend . . . and your Emily Ann."

   As he cocked a sad eye o'er a sheltering log,
   "Oh, a Glug is a Glug!" sighed the little red dog.

Printed in Australia
AUHW011836110122
358064AU00002B/3

9 781922 698094